P Divine
resence...

Melissa Giomi

Melissa Giomi
Facebook: @MelissaGiomiauthor
Instagram: @melissa.giomi

First Paperback Edition October 2025

ISBN 979-8-9933301-0-5 (paperback)
ISBN979-8-9933301-1-2 (ebook)

Library of Congress Control Number: 2025921223

Edited by Pia Edberg, piaedberg.com
Blurb by Book Blurb Magic, IG: @bookblurbmagic
Cover & interior design by Karolina Wudniak, karolinawudniak.com

Also by MELISSA GIOMI

Divine Encounters…

Divine Appointments…

Divine Whispers…

Table of Contents

He is Near

Where can I go from your Spirit?
Where can I flee from your presence?
If I go up to the heavens, you are there;
if I make my bed in the depths, you are there.
If I rise on the wings of the dawn,
if I settle on the far side of the sea,
even there your hand will guide me,
your right hand will hold me fast.
If I say, "Surely the darkness will hide me
and the light become night around me,"
even the darkness will not be dark to you;
the night will shine like the day,
for darkness is as light to you.

Psalm 139:7-12 NIV

Introduction

I'm delighted you found *Divine Presence...*, the fourth book in my Divine series— joining *Divine Encounters...*, *Divine Appointments...*, and *Divine Whispers...* on their journey into the world.

I am grateful these books give me the opportunity to share the healing, peace, and joy I have experienced as I live life with Jesus.

My prayer is that while you walk with me through *Divine Presence...*, you will discover the Divine all around you, as close as your next breath. May you feel His presence go before you each day and be with you when you close your eyes at night. Divine fingerprints as evidence of His love.

I hope you find exactly what you need in the pages of this book and are richly blessed. Peace be with you, along with my deepest gratitude for taking this journey with me.

He is Near

Joyful Noise

"THE HEAVENS declare the glory of God; the skies proclaim the work of his hands. Day after day they pour forth speech; night after night they reveal knowledge. They have no speech, they use no words; no sound is heard from them. Yet their voice goes out into all the earth, their words to the ends of the world." Psalm 19:1-4 NIV

The embers from last night's campfire spark and crackle in the crisp, early morning air. There is still a bit of warmth that reaches me. Memories of the stories told, the s'mores eaten, and easy comradery flit through my mind.

Steamy tendrils drift and wisp from my coffee. The peace of this early hour soothes and refreshes from a night of deep, cozy sleep. The haunting call of an owl and far-off yips of coyotes were my lullaby.

Tender, new sun rays hover and glisten off the dewy drops clinging to the Redwood trees, the gems of the forest. Beauty in simplicity, Creator's delight.

The scrub jays are the first to begin their chatter, soon joined by other light-dwellers as morning routines begin. Grey squirrels are bright-eyed and bushy-tailed as they forage and chatter the morning gossip.

Thin veils of mist rise up from the thick Redwood bark. The misty swirls and eddies look like elusive forest sprites as sunbeams catch them for a moment, then release them to vanish into the maze of branches and vines. Magical. Mysterious.

As the sun rises higher and its warmth penetrates the forest canopy, more of nature's choir join in the song: Chirps, croaks, chatter, and scolding echo through the trees. The rustles and cracks of disturbed undergrowth add to the harmony.

The voice of the forest is never truly silent. Creation blooms and swells with songs of delight and joy, rising up, up, up to His ears. The scent of old growth and fresh, bright pine mingle and blend with the nature songs—an incense of joy that wafts and twists upward in the crisp air, finding its way to the Holy of Holies.

Constant Companion

THE LORD REPLIED, "My Presence will go with you, and I will give you rest." Exodus 33:14 NIV

Each time I read this verse, I am comforted. I feel safe. Wherever life takes us, He WILL go with us. He goes before us to open up the way. He walks right beside us like a constant companion. He promises to give us rest. He is our burden-bearer and the One who carries us when we don't have the strength to take another step. Sometimes there is one set of footprints…

As a new day begins and your eyes flutter open, He is with you.

Enjoying the soothing warmth of hot coffee in your favorite mug, He is right there.

As daily appointments and to-do lists pop up, He's making a way through them.

The unexpected news that leaves you breathless and scared. He is there in the middle of it. You are tightly held against His heart as He speaks gentle words of healing and peace.

In the beauty of a sunset that dazzles you, He is with you, delighting in your joy and wonder.

When hurtful words that sting and wound are thrown like so much shrapnel, He is there picking up the pieces of your heart.

When you sprinkle compassion and kindness around you like glitter, He is there, replenishing your soul and filling you with blessings.

In the peace and refreshment you feel hiking through the Redwoods and soaking in the balm of nature, He is there, breathing life, love, and blessed rest into your weary soul.

Psalm 139:7 NIV "Where can I go from your Spirit? Where can I flee from your presence?"

Small Things

THE EARLY SUN filters through the blinds at the window. There's something gentle and delicate about those first rays of light. It feels hopeful.

The fluffy white cat finds a slash of sunlight on the carpet by the bookcase and settles in. He's had his breakfast and a bath, so it's time for his morning rest. The soft, grey and white cat finds her spot in the sun on the cozy, green blanket draped over the bed. Fully relaxed, she stretches out, tail gently flicking as she drifts off.

I hear the garden come alive as I sip my hot coffee. It's a simple thing that brings me happiness as I start my day. The earthy taste and warmth are soothing.

Red-brown squirrels chase each other through the patio and onto the wooden fence, where their race takes them onto the neighbor's roof and beyond. Joyful and full of energy.

The newly leafed apple tree is filled with red and gold finches, house sparrows, and soft grey doves. They watch as I fill the bird feeders and scatter seeds along the ground. A blue jay joins the crowd, eyeing the peanuts strewn among the flowers and bird baths. Soon, there will be gossipy chatter and scolding as they descend to peck, scratch, and kick, finding just the right seeds and other morsels for breakfast.

There is joy in the routine things that make up a given day.

A tinkling bell heralds the arrival of the neighborhood tomcat. He stops by every so often for his breakfast and a head rub.

As the morning progresses, I am at peace as I tend to the garden and inhale the fruity floral scent of the jasmine climbing the trellis, perfuming the morning air.

I sense You in the bright colors, the spicy, flowery scents, and the hope that the pale, lemony sunlight splashes onto the tree branches, dancing to the sweet tune of the tiny wind chime that tinkles and sings in the breeze.

We talk as I go about my morning routine. You speak kind and intimate things to my heart. You know the pleasure that these small things bring to my soul. It comforts me, making me feel seen and known. What a happy, life-giving way to begin each day; taking Your love and companionship with me everywhere my feet may go.

Road Map

Most of us have a morning routine that we like to follow. Mine is typically dictated by my cats. They have a routine and are not fans of any deviations. I'm not a fan of deviations from mine either. So, cats dealt with, coffee comes next as I prepare myself for what the day will hold.

As the last vestiges of sleep wear off and hot coffee brings its soothing comfort, I try to visualize what my day will bring. Wouldn't it be wonderful to have a roadmap laid out before us each morning, showing the twists, turns, and straightaways that our day will hold—the who, what, when? Would it make things easier in our planning and rehearsing? I wonder…

On the surface, I imagine feeling relief in knowing what's coming and when. No blindsiding jolt. No unexpected loss, failure, or hard conversations. Excited anticipation over something pleasant coming our way, a positive outcome, or a blessed time of rest.

However, a detailed map with every nuance exposed and laid bare for us opens doors to unwelcome traveling companions, like Fear, Anxiety, Overthinking, and Control. We would never feel prepared enough, ready enough, or well-equipped enough to tackle all that waits for us down the hill, around the bend, or in that long stretch of valley. A field day for Chaos, with our frantic attempts to manipulate or change the course of what we see coming.

Despite the fear of the unknown that we all wrestle with, wouldn't we miss the unexpected joy of stumbling upon hidden blessings or the relief of a conversation that goes better than planned? There is something beautiful and exciting about a day filled with twists and turns. Yes, some of those turns hold hard, frightening, heartbreaking things. But missing out on the surprise, delight, and peace when we make His presence our traveling companion is something I don't want to live without. The best roadmap is simply Him. He is the Light and the Whisper that leads and directs us on the path He has pre-equipped us to walk. He knows what each day holds and is the perfect Guide—our blessed assurance that all is well, that we are safe, and dearly loved.

The Lord replied, "My Presence will go with you, and I will give you rest." Exodus 33:14 NIV

FATHER,

I pray for the one who is wrestling with uncertainty. They are at a crossroads right now and have choices to make. Voices of friends and family are coming at them from all sides. Noise, chatter, and strong opinions are overwhelming, and they can't hear themselves think. They want so much to do the right thing, to follow You, and please You.

I pray that You will silence the noise and bring them out into a spacious place where they can rest their mind in stillness and peace. Give them a safe place to truly hear Your voice. You have guided them in the past, and You will do it again. Please speak to them in the unique way that You created them to hear Your voice. May they encounter You in intimate and startling ways as You reveal their next steps and show them how to proceed. Remind them that You are the Alpha and Omega, beginning and the end. You see their entire journey laid out before You. You know the way.

I pray this beloved one will trust You, will believe that they hear You calling them forward, and will respond with belief that You are for them. Thank you for filling them with confidence and purpose. Thank you for guiding them along the life-road You created for them.

In Your beautiful name, Jesus,
Amen

Isaiah 30:21 NIV "Whether you turn to the right or to the left, your ears will hear a voice behind you, saying, 'This is the way; walk in it.'"

Surprises

EARLY MORNING SUNLIGHT cheerfully illuminates the cozy kitchen in her cabin by the lake. A hot cup of Paris blend tea keeps her hands toasty. Steamy, hot oatmeal with brown sugar, walnuts, and golden raisins awaits. The embers from last night's fire snicker and glow, still giving off a bit of heat.

January at the cabin is chilly and peaceful. Dewdrops glint off the reeds standing guard at the edge of the lake. Sunlight sparkles off the frosted needles of the old pine that has stood as protector over the cabin for as long as she can remember. The many creatures that call the lake their home are still here prowling, hunting, and sunning themselves. The pace and rhythm of life slow a bit as Nature cozies into the slumber of Winter.

Charity feels her bunched-up shoulders and neck relax and release as she sits in the silence. Her tense body and racing mind need a reprieve. This is where she'll find it. "Help me find my way back to You," she whispers.

Charity has walked with Him for a long time, and she knows His voice, the gentle nudge that tugs at her soul. The songs and murmurs that whisper holy, divine things into her heart, speaking healing over her. "Come away…" they say.

Dressed in layers with hiking boots and a hat, Charity heads out for a walk around the lake. Filled with anticipation at the treasures and surprises she will come across, her heart is happy, and her steps are light. The crisp wintry air is rejuvenating as she breathes in deep and long, inhaling peace and exhaling heaviness. The mysterious, divine exchange she's been waiting for over these past few months. Rest. Peace. Hope.

As the leaf-strewn path veers down and to the right, she hears the lapping waves on the bank of the lake, moved along by a brisk, bright breeze. Rhythmic and soothing, the sound comforts and calms.

Further along, sunlight filters through the pine branches, leaving lovely patches of light and shadow along her route. A reminder that light always pierces the darkness. Nothing is hidden from Him. He will always find her, even when her life-journey leads through valleys and twisty paths that seem hopelessly dim and gloomy. Those who follow Him shall not walk in darkness…[1]

Around a sharp twist in the path, a small outcropping of rocks hugs the edge of the water. Reeds and other water plants grow along one side, creating the perfect hiding spot for crawdads and other small lake creatures. Footprints in the squishy mud at the edge of the lake—raccoons or perhaps an opossum looking for

---

1   John 8:12 NIV

a late-night nibble? Remnants of red, orange-y shells confirm it—the circle of life.

Sitting on the rocks, Charity soaks in the warmth of the wintry sun, inhaling that earthy lake smell that feels like home. His presence is strong here. The sights, sounds, and scents of the trees and lake are like beautiful gifts waiting for her to unwrap. How He knows her! The One who created all things hand-picked bits of joy, delight, and unexpected encounters with Himself to remind her that all is well. She is loved, and never alone.

Moving along, Charity tucks into her heart all the carefully placed blessings and treasures she encounters along the way. Reminders for when life gets messy and chaotic. The beauty of a sweet purple mountain flower that stubbornly holds on despite the cold slumber of winter. Antics of the scrub jays and squirrels dashing through blankets of pine needles, scolding each other, and making her laugh. Whiffs of old-Earth scents—timeless and eternal. Everything that speaks to Charity—safety, love, and being fully known—was intentionally scattered along her path this morning by the Father.

Back at the cabin, she relaxes on the deck in her comfy lounger, hot cocoa taking the chill from her hands. Her time with Jesus this morning was exactly what she needed—refreshed with treasured surprises and blessings to keep close to her heart.

As the sounds of the mountain lake stir, shush, and float over her, she gently drifts off to sleep in the winter sun.

Today

Soft, filtered light streams through the blinds, and a cool, comforting breeze floats through the open window. It's scented with honeysuckle and a faint hint of lemon balm. "Time to get up," it breathes. The first birdsong of the morning fills the garden. A beautiful way to wake up.

Hot coffee warms up my still-waking hands and mind; the first sip warm and soothing. Delicious! The cats impatient for breakfast, meow and fuss at my feet.

Today is a good day.

An early morning text from a soldier far away eases the worry that always hovers; a relief to know all is well. Pictures of grand-dogs and grand-cats from an adult child living a good life bring smiles and a lightness to the morning.

New growth on the bright spring flowers looks so joyful and happy. The red and yellow roses, catmint, and yarrow show off their vibrant palette of colors. The buzzing of bees and flitting hummingbirds feel purposeful and calming.

Today is a good day.

Pleasant greetings from other early morning walkers in the neighborhood set a friendly tone for the unfolding day. It means a lot to be seen and acknowledged.

An unexpected card in the mail from a friend "just because" is a sweet surprise. It's wonderful to be remembered when life feels unpredictable and lonely. It's easy to feel forgotten.

Today is a good day.

Stopping downtown for coffee and exchanging pleasantries with strangers while waiting in line is friendly and simple. Light banter and easy jokes boost energy and contentment. It's cheerful. Laughter is good for the soul.

Walking through the park enjoying the drowsy warmth of the afternoon, I spot a man and his brindle dog lying in the grass under a tree. It looks like life has been rough for him, and it tugs at my heart. He is a human created in the Father's likeness whom Jesus died for and loves unconditionally. A group of young men passes by and stops to talk to him. They pet his dog and offer him their Subway bag. There is still compassion and kindness in the world, even though it seems harder to find.

Today is a good day.

As the day winds down and night falls, the air has a chilly bite to it. The last vestiges of the day disappear with the setting sun. One last flare of light, and it is the moon's turn to ride high. The chorus of frogs and crickets begins, softly at first. Soon, it will be a full-blown nature symphony. The peacefulness falls and envelopes me. It feels safe and mysterious.

Reflecting on how this day unfolded, I feel a swell of gratitude for the way my Father guided me throughout the day. His presence infused every interaction, comment, and smile that was filtered through His hands. What a compassionate, all-powerful, and unfailing Father! I am His and He is mine.

Today was a good day.

Psalm 118:24 NLT "This is the day the Lord has made. We will rejoice and be glad in it."

Perfect Love

HAVE YOU EVER EXPERIENCED the disconnected, fearful feeling of being far from God? Wondering if He has withdrawn His love and attention because of something you have or have not done? These feelings are sly and insidious, latching onto our hearts and minds. Feeding off the insecurity they produce, they steadily rob us of the intimate, precious peace and unconditional love that only comes from Him.

As we feel this perceived distance between us and Jesus grow, we may unconsciously punish ourselves by withdrawing and denying ourselves closeness with Him. Feeling like we are lacking, not good enough, and unworthy, we focus on performing, earning, and striving for His love and attention, even though we already have it. Can you see how this vicious circle of performance captures us, rendering us vulnerable, exhausted, and fearful?

God is love. He is perfect. He is unfailing and omnipotent. In His sovereignty, love, and compassion, He sees through the striving straight to the heart that is weary, hurting, and in need of His perfect rest and peace. He created each of us knowing our capacity to fail, get it wrong, and just be human. He *doesn't need* us to do anything to earn His love, favor, and attention. He wants to wrap us up, enfold us into Himself, and tend to our messy hearts reminding us that fear is the opposite of love.

"There is no fear in love. But perfect love drives out fear, because fear has to do with punishment. The one who fears is not made perfect in love." 1 John 4:18 NIV.

If you feel overwhelmed, tired, and far from Him right now; if His voice seems muted and distorted, speak His name. He never distances Himself. He's right there. Can you feel Him wrapping you up? Can you hear His voice saying, "Welcome back, beautiful child?" Ask Him to cover you and nestle you into Him. He will do it. He's never stopped.

FATHER,

I pray for the one who needs to know that You see them. Circumstances have left them feeling disconnected and invisible. They don't know what to do with the hurt and insecurity, Father. It hovers over all they do and taints even the good days with a bitter and acrid taste they can't shake. It is painful to feel unseen and anonymous.

I pray that You will sing Your songs of acceptance, love, and attention over them. Banish the heaviness that attempts to steal their joy and peace.

I pray they will see the light of Your unconditional love breaking through the murk and cloudiness. May the light fall on them and bring them into Your presence, where all darkness must flee.

I pray the one You love will encounter You in a beautiful and unique way as You comfort their soul and pour Your healing over them. Assure them that You see them, intimately know them, and deeply love them.

I pray that they will stay a while in Your arms, allowing You to heal, cleanse, and restore their confidence that they are who You say they are—chosen, blessed, loved, fully known, and completely seen.

In the healing name of Jesus Christ,
Amen

Psalm 139:17-18 NLT "How precious are your thoughts about me, O God. They cannot be numbered! I can't even count them; they outnumber the grains of sand! And when I wake up, you are still with me!"

Deep in the Woods

THERE'S A MYSTERIOUS PLACE deep in the woods. It's far off the beaten path where no human has ventured. Untouched. Pure nature.

No boot prints are found, but there are footprints. Forest dwellers.

Creature paths appear random and meandering, but they are not. These trails are specific and intentional. They know where their food comes from and the safest way to get there. Provision. Trust.

Nestled into a craggy rock formation high on a forested slope, a spring bubbles up and over the roots and rocks, splashing its way down. It's been bubbling and sparkling for years. Following a well-worn route along the forest floor, the stream bed weaves its way through gullies, towering pines, aspens, and mountain meadows. Sometimes the clear water tumbles and crashes over various forest debris, faster and faster as it descends. Other times, it slows and spreads, creating deep pools of cool water that laze along, peacefully chattering in swirls and eddies. Life-giving.

The absence of humans doesn't mean the absence of sound. The deep woods are a sound garden of their own. Nature has a voice, and it's primeval and beautiful.

The pines and aspens shiver and whisper with the wind as it sighs through branches and moves along tree trunks, creaking and bending—a symphony of sorts.

Sticks, dead leaves, and pine needles rustle and snap as unseen creatures forage and spy under fallen trees and twisting vines.

The babble of birdsong in the forest canopy sounds chaotic at first listen. But the trills, melodies, and harmonies blend into an exciting and joyful concerto that echoes through the trees, along the stream, and over the meadows.

Nightfall has its own unique orchestra. Whispery feathers blend with the haunting call of the owl in flight; it is otherworldly and beautiful. The stealthy sounds of night hunters and creepers as they prowl, hide, and call are eerie and supernatural.

This untouched slice of nature is a beautiful testament to Divine creation. The One who created all things sees and hears the happenings in the deep woods. It brings Him joy in its purity. The creaks and shushing of the wind in the canopy, rushing water, and the groans of nature are like a symphony of worship. His creation cries out to Him with joyful noises and complete trust in His provision. It is pleasing incense and a thing of deep beauty to Him who sits on the throne. Devoid of human voices, even the rocks cry out to the Father who holds the world in His hands.

Psalm 150:6 NLT "Let everything that breathes sing praises to the Lord! Praise the Lord!"

Everlasting Arms

SOMETIMES living with faith feels like walking a tightrope. On days when circumstances align with my carefully laid plans, the rope feels wide and close to the ground; it's easy to hop down if a small deviation pops up on the path ahead. I'm in control, I've got this.

But then come the days when my plans do not go the way I carefully plotted and rehearsed. Unexpected enemies like Distraction, Fear, Pride, Anger, and Loss appear—unwelcome and unplanned. Blindsided. My tightrope of self-reliance becomes taut and narrow. Panic and Chaos glide in with their mocking snickers and disorienting chatter, reminding me that I can't see the ground. I'm too high up. What if I fall?

Precariously balancing on this thin, rigid rope of Faith, I notice a lovely fragrance wafting and swirling up from beneath me. It smells like peace and safety. Love. Gingerly, I peek down and there, gently fluttering and settling in the breeze, are beautiful feathers like a safety net of wings. Everlasting arms. Heavenly breath buoys me up, keeping my feet straight and steady. Courage and strength, not from my own understanding, gently infuse my mind and spirit. You speak peace to my heart and hope to my soul, as my enemies slink and fade away.

"Steady on, girl!" I hear joy in Your voice, and it gives me confidence. I am safe with your wings below me. Everlasting arms ready to catch and carry me. I am sure-footed with Your Light before me. Like a good Shepherd, you lead me through hills and valleys, over high mountain peaks, and safely through deep ravines. When circumstances and world events weigh heavily, You lift that weight, reminding me that not everything is mine to hold.

Whatever terrain I find myself navigating and however narrow the road, You set my feet on that path before the world was born. Nothing is hidden from You, and all will be exposed to the Light.

Wrapped in this knowledge, I lean into the Everlasting arms of Jesus.

"The eternal God is your refuge, and underneath are the everlasting arms. He will drive out your enemies before you, saying, 'Destroy them!'" Deuteronomy 33:27 NIV

The Road Not Chosen

Isn't it amazing that before we were born, God perfectly mapped out the twisty, windy road that would be our life journey? He carefully planned for every mountain, valley, and stretch of road, equipping us with exactly what we need for each roadblock we navigate and person we meet. He leaves nothing to chance. It's all divinely orchestrated, this seemingly chaotic, yet beautifully crafted planet populated with humanity that is messy, precious, delightful, and completely known. Loved.

It doesn't catch Him off guard when we worry, rehearse, and stress over our future. He knows we have plans, ideas, and dreams because He placed them in us. He omnipotently sees the path we need to follow to accomplish the purpose we were created to fulfill. Our journeys brush up against others following the road set out before them. Interwoven with blessings and kindness. A human tapestry that He calls His masterpiece.

I wonder, if like me, you question why and how you ended up on the road you are traveling. Sometimes it's smooth, easy, and all is going your way. Other times it is not. You know the dreams and passions you have inside that are bursting to get out. You have things to do and places to go, but the road you are walking is not the one you would have chosen. The obstacles you have to overcome—pain, loss, loneliness, and fear—seem to serve no purpose. They feel so heavy on your shoulders. So tired, so weary...where is this road leading? How much longer do you have to struggle through?

I wonder if gratitude is the answer. It seems completely counterintuitive. It feels wrong and dismissive of the hardships, but maybe it isn't? When I look back on my life, there are portions of my road that I disliked to my core. Seasons that filled me with fear, anger, physical and mental pain, and sadness. I saw no blessings there. I saw nothing to be thankful for, and I did not feel any gratitude for what I had to slog through. It felt pointless and mean.

I did make it through that season of life, but not without scars and memories. I wasn't filled with the joy of the Lord or brimming with thankfulness. Definitely not. It was a road that I would not have chosen. But...

Now that I am past that part of my journey, I can look back and see that things played out the way they needed to. Those difficult sections of the path were necessary. Never minimizing or dismissive of the pain, but it is part of my life story. He holds my tears in lovely crystal jars, continually speaking blessings, prophesy, healing, and peace over them.

The lessons learned about God's faithfulness, goodness, mercy, and healing needed to happen the way they did. Not everything turned out the way I hoped and dreamed, and He has helped me wrestle with that loss and disappointment. It is a blessing to know that parts of my life story have brought hope and healing to others who needed to see that scars can be beautiful, reminders that there is always light in the darkest of nights. The pain and obstacles others have faced have done the same for me. All interconnected and planned to bless and heal—a revelation of Himself. God does dwell in and bless the broken road that in our finite human wisdom we would not have chosen.

FATHER,

Today, I pray for the one who feels stuck. Life feels mundane and ordinary. No major catastrophe is raging, and no health or financial issues are looming over them. Things feel stagnant as fear and anxiety whisper that they are missing the mark, not hearing Your voice. They need clarity and direction. I ask that You remind Your dear one that You are the Author and Creator of their life-story, and You are not finished.

The journey You set in motion for them before they took their first breath is rich and complex. It's full of twists, turns, and slow-paced seasons that allow them to refresh and gain knowledge for the seasons still to come. Please sing over them the songs their heart needs to receive in this season of rest, refreshment, and simple, but holy time spent with You. Any time spent in communion with You is divine. It's holy ground. Fill them with Your presence as they wait in anticipation for the divine appointments You have placed along their life-path.

In the holy name of Jesus Christ,
Amen

Jeremiah 29:11 NIV "For I know the plans I have for you," declares the Lord, "plans to prosper you and not to harm you, plans to give you hope and a future."

Be Still

It's 3:00 AM at the little house on the corner of Route 16 and Mountain House Road. The leftover embers from last night's fire in the sturdy, squat woodstove glow and flicker. Vestiges of warmth still permeate the living room. Vegas, the black and tan Rottweiler, gently snores on his comfy bed while Thomas, the tabby cat, peers out the front window into the blackness of the night.

Lyndee is restless again. Sleep is elusive. Her cozy house is so quiet that the silence seems to echo in on itself. The only sounds are the far-off train whistle as it chugs through town and the lonely cry of a hunting owl. Those are comforting sounds which usually help her drift off to sleep, but not tonight. Her mind will not settle. There are too many voices in her head vying for attention.

The voice of Anxiety pulls her to revisit all the hard conversations she's had in the past few months. Was she rude? Was it okay to set boundaries to protect her peace, her safety, her worth? Then comes the voice of Fear, reminding her of past experiences that left her broken, wounded, and fragile. "Are you ever truly safe?" it sighs. These fearful thoughts mix and mingle with the voice of Condemnation that whispers and spits harsh words, judgment, and vicious lies that her life is of no value. Not good enough.

All this wrestling, managing, and trying to cope has left her exhausted. "I'm so tired, I can't do this anymore."

The words slip from her lips and float to His ears. Compassion and deep, mysterious, supernatural love gently descend on strands of Hope to Lyndee's aching heart. Victory joins Hope and silences the voices that do not belong to the heavenly realm. They flee at His word, His glance, His command. Peace and Rest follow Hope down the swirling cord connecting Lyndee to the One who loves her most. In her heart, she hears His voice speak to her. Deep calls to deep, ministering, healing, and binding up wounds. "Be still, He says, I am here, and I will give you rest."

Psalm 62:5 NIV "Yes, my soul, find rest in God; my hope comes from him."

Hope is Coming

THE DEEP WINTER chill stretches and spreads its tendrils of cold along rooftops, fence boards, and bare tree branches. Creatures burrow a bit deeper into nests padded with leaves, feathers, and tufts of fur they've gathered during their daylight adventures.

The neighborhood tabby cat stalks the garden in search of a late-night snack amongst the ground cover and garden statues.

Finger-like wisps of clouds sail high in the winter sky, obscuring the moon and constellations as they are blown and shifted as He directs them.

Vestiges of leftover holiday lights wink and gleam in the chill darkness of the quiet neighborhood. Holiday nostalgia lingers. It is hard to let go of the high expectations each Christmas season brings. The hope that things will be different this year with careful planning to ensure all the holiday things are attended to and accomplished. So much disappointment when things do not turn out the way we dreamed they would.

As dawn rises over the chilly winter morning, its tender light beams peep over the horizon. Soft light gently touches the frozen, icy places, causing them to sparkle and shine—a thing of beauty. Tendrils of misty vapor, like prayers mingled with Holy breath, rise from the iced-over places carried upward by heavenly songs. Beauty from darkness. The warmth of the Light guides and welcomes these prayers as a promise of His presence. Hope is coming for us. He is always coming.

The dark chill in a season of winter cannot hide us from Him. Blessings will keep pouring from His lips, and healing will keep flowing from His hands. His thoughts towards us will always be good. Dawn will always break through the darkness.

"But for you who fear my name, the Sun of Righteousness will rise with healing in his wings. And you will go free, leaping with joy like calves let out to pasture." Malachi 4:2 NLT

God in a Box

WHAT DOES YOUR BOX look like? The one you try to stuff God into so that He fits just right into the plans you have for your life. My box is decorated with nature things and brilliant colors. Inside my God-box are mementos of all He has done for me, road maps, and lists—my maps and my lists. I love lists and have plenty of them in the box, outlining what should be happening, how, with whom, and all those list-like details. Then the maps—well-marked so the Lord can easily see where and when I believe my life should go. All carefully detailed and organized. Not surprisingly, my lists and maps don't include hardships, valleys, and unanswered prayers.

I like to talk to Jesus when I'm outside, sipping my hot coffee, watching the garden wake up. I feel close to Him in nature, and that brings me peace. Recently, I was sitting on my patio mulling over certain circumstances and specific relationships when I began treading into Overthinking territory—a place that I am all too familiar with. As I worked hard to map out and list my next steps, those pesky thoughts that follow hard on the heels of Overthinking—worry, fear, control, and self-reliance—appeared. None of my plans, careful lists, and tedious mapping felt secure, safe, or solid. They felt frail, puny, and inadequate. My plans were full of holes and blank spaces that I just couldn't predict. It was frustrating that God wasn't fitting nicely into the careful box I prepared for Him, full of the answers that I wanted on my schedule.

As I was wrestling with these ideas churning in my mind, the wind chimes began tinkling with the breeze. "Remember..." they whispered as the wind floated along my shoulders, "I know the plans I have for you..."

As I watched the birds and critters scampering and fussing at the feeders, I noticed that they were well provided for. They trust that provision will be there when they need it. The cheerful flowers in the garden bloom where they are planted. They do not choose where they are carefully placed, but they still do what they are created to do. They bloom, are pruned, and nourished by the Master Gardener. These flowers don't complain, plan ahead, or fret over where they will be next year. No. They live in this season, in this moment.

Nature always gives me a new perspective. If He cares about flowers blooming in their assigned seasons, and about bluebirds finding the nourishment they need, how much more He will provide and care for me.

Isaiah 55:8-9 NLT settled in my mind as I rested in His presence.

"My thoughts are nothing like your thoughts," says the Lord. "And my ways are far beyond anything you could imagine. For just as the heavens are higher than the earth, so my ways are higher than your ways and my thoughts higher than your thoughts."

He is fierce, mysterious, and perfect. He can't be contained, tamed, or predicted. No box has ever held Him. The grave couldn't. Oh, the arrogance in thinking that I ever could…

"For through him God created everything in the heavenly realms and on earth. He made the things we can see and the things we can't see—such as thrones, kingdoms, rulers, and authorities in the unseen world. Everything was created through him and for him. He existed before anything else, and he holds all creation together." Colossians 1:16-17 NLT

Human arrogance is a dangerous thing; forgive me, Jesus. This box that I foolishly created to contain the Great I AM, I am turning into an altar that I will kneel before. All the mementos of miracles, the impossible that He made possible, the healing, the love, the precious, soul-deep conversations meant for He and I alone, will decorate this box-turned altar. Inside will be my soul perfectly contained within Him, safely guarded, deeply loved, and cherished as His precious treasure.

"Let the morning bring me word of your unfailing love, for I have put my trust in you. Show me the way I should go, for to you I entrust my life." Psalm 143:8 NIV

But God Says

HAVE YOU EVER STOPPED to think in a typical day, how many voices continuously vie for a place of prominence in your mind and spirit? It's prime real estate, and the battle is non-stop. Do you listen to the loud, harsh, defeating clamor or take a breath and carefully seek the gentle, kind whisper?

Insistent and insidious, Anxiety and Worry are a relentless team in the way they stir up and hint at bad things to come. Insinuating that circumstances will never be resolved, they taint daily living with vague feelings of unease, calamity, and pervasive all-or-nothing thinking.

Exhaustion and Overthinking team up with these two and scurry in, never allowing the mind to rest. They dig up past failures to ruminate over and relive with nagging thoughts of the future that hound and burrow in deep. They whisper that you are not enough and never will be. Failure. Lost cause. No hope.

This is the opening that Fear seeks to burst into the mix. Fear can be loud and bold, demanding attention as it amplifies those things that Worry and Anxiety bring to the forefront. "You aren't enough, try harder, you'll never be safe," it shouts. Plotting and scheming, Fear uses your desperate self-reliance in an attempt to isolate and close you off to the Voice that calls you beloved, worthy, masterpiece.

But God says,

"I am here. I love you. I see you. My precious child, I see all these things that keep you up at night, preventing you from seeing goodness, feeling safe, and accepting love, from seeing Me. I know what you fear and why you fear it. I was there when that terrible thing happened, when cruel words were spoken that broke your heart, when you made the mistake that you believe can never be redeemed. The silent tears you let no one see—I see them and save them. I will redeem them."

"I know everything about you, and here I am. You cannot cause Me to turn from you. When you breathe, I am the breath in your lungs. Place all the worry, fear, emotions, and those things you can't describe with words at My feet. I am your strong tower. I am your shelter and your peace. My presence soothes, heals, and silences those voices of evil, casting out fear and all enemies of your soul. They have no place in My presence. You are My temple where I dwell and will remain, if you allow Me in. Call on Me—My name is enough." This is what God says.

Proverbs 18:10 NIV "The name of the Lord is a fortified tower; the righteous run to it and are safe."

FATHER,

I pray for the one whose anxious thoughts are stealing their joy and drowning out peace. As they go about their day, scenarios of loss, fear, and panic threaten to overwhelm them. It chokes and constricts. They try to process all of these heavy feelings alone, try to suck it up and be strong, but it just causes more overwhelm. It is out of their control. Lord, this sweet one knows in their mind that You are the Prince of peace, Jehovah Shalom, but that knowledge isn't reaching their heart and soul.

Fear causes chaos, and self-reliance feeds doubt, while Panic triggers overthinking and isolation. Father, I pray that You break through all of these lies and schemes of the enemy. Silence the voices that are not from You. You are King of Kings and Lord of Lords. Hold them close and cover them with Your wings. Unbind their heart and soul from the chains of anxiety. Free them to hear the heavenly songs and healing that You are singing over them right now. You came to free captives and heal wounded hearts, and that includes them. May Your gentle Voice of love, joy, and rest fall on them. Restore their peace and refill their cup with joy and trust as they sit at Your feet and soak in Your presence.

In the mighty name of Jesus Christ,
Amen

Matthew 11:28-29 NLT "Then Jesus said, 'Come to me, all of you who are weary and carry heavy burdens, and I will give you rest. Take my yoke upon you. Let me teach you, because I am humble and gentle at heart, and you will find rest for your souls.'"

The Healing Place

THERE'S AN OLD wooden bridge in the forest. It spans a small creek that bubbles up from a spring high in the woods.

The hike to the bridge is remote and a bit lonely. I like it that way. Peace and solitude are what I seek.

Towering pines keep the path shaded and a little mysterious.

The rustling shush of the breeze in the canopy is comforting in a spiritual way—otherworldly.

If you're quiet and aware, you can feel His presence.

Bird song and creature chatter soothe my soul; shoulders relax, breathing deepens, hands unclench. Safe.

The crunching forest floor under my boots is steady, rhythmic, and purposeful. I know where I'm going—the healing place.

As I go further into the forest, the frenetic chaos of humanity sloughs off. My soul has room to breathe, to hope, and permission to feel.

My senses are heightened as nature gently cleanses and refreshes all that has been silenced, dulled, and dimmed.

Far off, stirring and scrabbling in the underbrush—I'm not alone here. Your presence silences and stills the Fear that tries to intercept and distract from the holy work You are doing. You aren't tame, but you're safe. Protector.

I see the bridge up ahead on the twisty path. I'm drawn to it. I'm here.

I sit on the old boards of the bridge spanning the chattering creek. The melody is joyful as it splashes over rocks and branches. It's filled with expectation and hope.

As I sit, Your divine whispers descend over me, restoring all that was lost, maimed, and shrouded by life; things I feared were out of reach and not for me.

Time is suspended as I am covered by the sounds of Your creation. I find You and You heal me. You sing to me that I am enough.

Deep calls to deep here in the woods. Seeking and finding. It's divine mystery and holy ground. This is the healing place.

Windswept

FALL DEEPENS into Winter. Fallen leaves, dry, crackly, and spent, gather in corners of the garden. Finished bits of autumn-blooming flowers and shrubs shed their stalks and petals. The plants settle in for a time of rest and deeper, quiet growth.

Russet squirrels and bright finches rustle and scritch in the piles and mounds of Fall's remnants. Nuts and seeds are gathered and buried. His creatures know the rhythms of nature.

The wintry sun tries to peek through the steel-grey clouds that speed across the sky, tumbling into one another as the wind directs their course.

On the patio, the misty air catches the steam from Vanessa's mug of hot tea and dances it up and around in spirals and whirls. She watches its wild, untamed dance, wishing that the heavy thoughts in her tired mind would be swept up high and away…

The happy, jingly wind chimes scattered around the patio spin and sing more vigorously as a bright, fresh wind picks up. Refreshing and crisp.

Turning her face into the brisk wind, Vanessa feels that invigorating rush of chilly air take her breath away. It feels freeing, fierce, and bold.

The playful eddies and gusts stir the leaves and garden detritus, sending it skipping and dashing through the patio, up and over her, catching in her blowing hair and on the sleeves of her worn green hoodie.

She watches the finished petals, leaves, and spent things being blown out and away; corners and hiding places exposed to the cleansing breath of the wind.

Quietly watching the wind scour the garden nooks and crannies, Vanessa senses Him. His breath is like a strong, stiff, healing wind whipping away fears, worries, doubts, and disappointment. Where the Spirit of the Lord is, there is freedom…

Deep inhalations invite His Spirit to cleanse and refresh her world-weary mind and body. Such peace. Such love. She is bathed in His breath and healed by His Spirit.

Secret Things

FILTERED SUNLIGHT seeps through the branches of the willow tree sheltering the bench by the edge of the pond. It feels gentle and kind, a balm to her soul.

Pond creatures stir and murmur to themselves as they stretch—time for breakfast. The early sunlight reaches the jumbled-up rocks along the edge of the pond where the turtles like to sun themselves. They keep a sharp eye on the goings-on.

A green heron has commenced fishing, patiently waiting in the reeds for breakfast to stir. He is soon joined on the opposite side of the pond by a white heron searching for the crawdads and tiny fish that inhabit the muddy edges.

Restless nights with little sleep wear on her. Certain scenarios play over and over in her mind. If she could just figure out the next steps and see a bit of the future, that would make everything right, wouldn't it? The uncertainty is frustrating and fragile. It feels out of control and precarious. She has to let this worry go. Help, Jesus.

Sitting in the peace and gentleness of this lovely morning, she hears the cows lowing in the open space across the way. Their voices mix with the calls of red-winged blackbirds, fussy geese, and gossipy ducks—soothing and restful.

Busy and active, the pond dwellers slip, glide, and fly, watching and waiting for their next meal in tune with creation. Nature follows its routines and primal, ingrained patterns, fully trusting that its needs will be met.

As her heart and mind quiet, nature begins to heal her. Jesus is here with her on the bench under the budding willow tree. He speaks rest and safety to her spirit through the sights, sounds, and scents of the little pond. The wind whispers of sacred, secret things as it puffs and chases itself through the reeds and tree branches. "Cast your cares…" it sings.

As she rests in His peace, He speaks hope to her burdened heart. She and her loved ones are safe with Him. He knows. He sees them. The future is His, and He dwells there in it. Those secret, hidden things belong to Him alone. She can relax and enjoy the journey with Him, trusting that He will open up the way before her and those she holds so dear. He will cover them with His wings. The Light in the darkness, the Keeper of secrets. All will be revealed in His perfect timing. He knows the plans He has…

"He reveals deep and mysterious things and knows what lies hidden in darkness, though he is surrounded by light." Daniel 2:22 NLT

Need and Want

I LIKE TO START my mornings with hot, steamy coffee, talking to Jesus. The conversation isn't always deep and theological; often it's not. Sometimes our talks consist of me commenting on my garden and the bright, cheerful colors, or thanking Him for the gorgeous sunrise and the unique way He filters the light through the tree branches. Like a treasure hunt, I look forward to discovering all the ways He sets up the morning just for me. He does it for you, too. I feel loved, special, and wanted. Wanted. Not needed.

There's a sweet, intimate feeling that comes with knowing that you are wanted and not needed. Being needed isn't a bad thing. But for humanity, need often comes with expectations attached. Someone needs you to find a solution, needs you to take them somewhere, needs you to show up, take on, and fix whatever it might be. Sometimes another person's *need* really isn't ours to carry.

Jesus supplies all of our needs. He gives wisdom and discernment when there is a fork in the road, and I have choices to make. He provides safety and protection when threats appear, and I'm helpless to defend myself. He equips me with just enough to arrive at the end of each day—what I need when I need it.

As I stood in my garden thinking about this, I realized that not only do I need Him, but I want Him. I want to spend time with Him. I need to know that, in times of loneliness when I feel overlooked, forgotten, and passed over, He never leaves me and always has His eye on me. Apple of His eye. Perfect friend. It's a wonderful thing to know that He loves to delight and surprise me with the very things He created me to love and crave. When I'm world-weary, I want to rest in His strong arms and know that I have permission to stay; I'm not a burden.

What a deep and mysterious love. I will never fully understand it this side of heaven, but I want it. I simply want more of Him. He wants me, and He wants you.

Jesus doesn't need me. There is nothing I can do or handle for Him. I bring no skills that He lacks or wisdom that He seeks. All I can bring is myself. He loves me. He wants me. I am enough for Him. So are you.

Psalm 13:5-6 NLT "But I trust in your unfailing love. I will rejoice because you have rescued me. I will sing to the Lord because he is good to me."

Psalm 18:19 NIV "He brought me out into a spacious place; he rescued me because he delighted in me."

FATHER,

Please gently lift and tightly hold the one who feels left out and passed over. They want so much to fit in, to be liked, sought out, and included. The pain of being overlooked is real, and it hurts. They try hard to justify and dismiss the wounds through busyness and self-deprecation, but the pain leaks out through silent tears that no one sees. No one but You.

Please tenderly hold this dear one. Speak Your words of life, belonging, and unconditional love straight to their spirit. You are their best friend, closer than a brother. You created them exactly how they are meant to be, and no one can take that from them. You do not make mistakes. I pray You will bring good things, divine purpose, and joy to their hearts as they navigate this season of loneliness. May they cling to You and look to You for their validation and peace. Thank you for the deep love You hold for them. Thank you for healing their aching heart.

In the compassionate name of Jesus,
Amen

Proverbs 18:24 NIV "One who has unreliable friends soon comes to ruin, but there is a friend who sticks closer than a brother."

He Walks with Me

THE SANDY PARKING LOT is empty this morning except for a few scattered cars. This is my favorite beach. The breeze carries the sounds of happy, barking dogs fetching driftwood and balls thrown out into the ocean; owners in bright-colored windbreakers and beanies clapping and calling as the game is repeated.

The seabirds have been up since dawn, calling and wheeling over the beach and shallows. Sharp eyes find tiny crabs and other crustaceans for breakfast. Their calls hold a tinge of loneliness and a wild sense of freedom. I feel oddly envious of it.

Making my way down the steep steps to the beach, I feel the energy and power of the waves pulling at me to come closer, listen, and immerse myself in their fierce wildness. It's exhilarating!

With a heady sense of anticipation, I make my way to where the waves break and wash out with swirling eddies and haphazard currents depositing their treasures onto the beach. Gifts from the deep.

The breeze off the ocean is stiff and bracing. It cleanses. Filling my lungs with the pure, chilled, briny air, it begins to loosen and free my mind, soul, and body. Muscles release their tension. Overthinking has no place here. It's liberating! Freedom. Healing.

Walking along the edge of the water in the firm, wet sand, I know I am not alone. I feel You everywhere and right next to me all at once. Your presence is living, breathing, and powerful. I need You. You see the worries, fears, and striving that attach themselves tightly to my mind and spirit, bound there by unbelief, self-reliance, and the constant wondering if I'm enough. You take the lies and shouts that work so hard to silence Your voice and throw them to the winds and waves that obey Your command; removed from me as far as the East is from the West. I feel light and hopeful. Safe. Protected. Loved.

Moving along the beach, my mind is open and uncluttered. Clear. I talk to You. You hear me. Whispers, shouts, and deep tears from hidden places flow freely. You see me, and the need, and the love. You sing over me in heavenly languages. It isn't too much. I'm not too much. You don't leave. You walk with me. You heal me.

Up ahead, along the base of the craggy cliffs, I see a sheltered space and make my way to it. It's protected and tucked in from the stiff, bracing winds and salty spray. There is a bubbly trickle of water flowing down the grooves in the cliff wall. It's calming. Gentle and delightful. I envision myself safe and wrapped up in Your arms. We sit there for a while, just You and I. Warmth, sea scents, and peace permeate and dance around us; Your presence filling all the empty spaces in me.

Corner Café

THERE'S A CAFÉ on the corner of Elm and Franklin. Rustic and charming. Its old, wood-hewn sign swings and creaks if the wind picks up. One wall has floor-to-ceiling windows with a great view of the little shops and ice cream parlor to the right and the leafy, flower-filled park to the left. Shade trees and the happy, tinkling fountain bring peace and rest to those who venture in to sit for a bit.

The tables and comfy chairs invite quiet reading or cozy conversations; never rushed. This vibe of safety, kindness, and welcome makes one feel seen in this busy, self-centered world. Restful acoustic guitar music plays softly in the background. An array of locally made pastries, cookies, and granola adds to the rustic, homey feel of the place. The coffee is a special roast made just for the café by a local coffee roaster—Holy Grounds blend.

The Corner Café has been around for years, passing down through Brian's family for as long as he can remember. Coffee is in the blood! More importantly is the family's desire for their community to have a place to call home where they are seen, known, and appreciated. "Just love people and let God sort the rest," his grandpa Ed always said.

Seeing the regulars stop in at the same time, order the same thing, and sit in the same spot makes him smile. It feels good to make others happy and feel valued. It never gets old seeing their faces light up as he asks after their grandchildren, the garden, various pets, and checks in on their health, and whatever else is going on in their lives. Each day, Brian prays before opening the doors, asking the Lord to grant him the wisdom, compassion, and discernment he needs to speak life, love, and belonging into each soul he encounters. He prays that his café will be a holy and healing ground for those who enter. He wants them to feel His presence.

Business is brisk this morning. The gorgeous weather has more people out than usual. Many stop by for their daily chat to share a few stories, grab their coffee to go, and head to the park. Maria, one of his regulars, stops in for her Chai Latte with whip, a dash of cinnamon, and a Morning bun to go. "Brian," she says, "Jesus is up to something today. I can feel it in my bones and on the back of my neck." Grabbing her order, she finds a shady bench in the park and pulls out her book.

Hmmm, he wonders. *Hmmm…*

The small bell above the door jingles and sings. Glancing up, Brian notices a man he hasn't seen before looking around as he walks up to the counter. Kindness. The sensation of kindness flows off of this stranger, permeating the air around him. Tall, but unassuming, he scans the menu on the back wall, then stoops a bit to look in the pastry cases. His voice, as he orders a large, black, Holy Grounds blend and granola with berries and honey, is rich and full. Soothing. Safe. The stranger takes his order to a table along the far wall with a view of the park. As he settles in, Brian can't stop watching him, drawn to the deep kindness emanating from this man.

As the morning wears on, Brian watches in fascination as locals and strangers alike stop by the café and somehow end up talking to this man. Some exchange quick, jaunty banter and pleasant conversation, while others linger at His table, words and emotions flowing freely—known, heard, and loved. What each person has in common is the way they leave this stranger. Some appear lighter and finally able to breathe. Others radiate joy and peace. Still others have a sheen of tears in their eyes and on their cheeks. How beautiful they look! Healed. Whole.

As the day winds down and the Corner Café empties, Brian watches as the stranger, the last to leave, walks past each table. His fingers gently trace whirls and symbols along the top of each one. His whispered words float and fall, hovering over each chair and countertop like a covering. Sacred. Supernatural.

As He reaches the door, the stranger turns to Brian and looks at him. A feeling of peace and being deeply known washes over him, enfolding him in a gentle but fiercely protective love. As the door clicks closed, Brian hears the faintly whispered words, "Holy ground…" floating in the air behind Him. A divine exchange took place in his café today.

Before turning out the lights and locking up for the night, Brian makes one last sweep of the café. Passing the tables, he notices words lightly etched in a beautiful script at the left corner of each tabletop. Love. Joy. Peace. Patience. Kindness. Goodness. Faithfulness. Gentleness. Self-Control.

Chapel in the Woods

THERE IS A LITTLE CHAPEL in the Redwoods. It is deep in the forest along a narrow, off-the-beaten-path trail. Tucked underneath a canopy of clustered old-growth trees, the forest has accepted the chapel as one of its own, the way it is sheltered and hidden away. The silence of this little grove is like a holy hush as only nature and the Divine speak here.

Gentle, filtered light bathes the steep roof, highlighting the moss and lichen that cover it.

Tall stained-glass windows with cracked and weathered wooden sills welcome the sunrise in the East. The light casts a holy glow of muted purples, blues, and reds along the simple wooden pews and the rough-hewn altar.

Hand-carved double doors, slightly off-kilter, creak in welcome to the one who enters.

His Spirit dwells here in this simple, hidden chapel; a palpable presence of sacred mystery. Those who seek refuge, peace, and rest find it—a Divine invitation. Hurts are healed and tears are caught, wounds are bound, and answers sought. Holy breath speaks life and rebukes those things that have no place here. This is holy ground.

Ahhh, the things these old trees have seen and heard as weary wanderers discover the little chapel in the woods. They are drawn by Divine whispers and the need to find solace and love, the need to find Him. Chains breaking, hearts mended, victory shouted, and deep pain healed. Nature and the Divine intertwined in a holy and sacred dance of healing and peace. The Healer enthroned in a simple old chapel nestled in the midst of His creation.

Boundaries

EARLY SUNLIGHT starts its upward journey, peeking over the roof of the neighbor's patio. Stretching and relishing in the coziness of my blankets, I force myself to get up. It will be another day full of errands, appointments, and all the things that people cram into the 24 hours of a given day. Expectations.

My cherished morning routine is rushed and fussy. The comforting warmth of my coffee and the joy of watching the garden wake up feel hurried and half-hearted. Anxiety hovers in the background—hurry up! Don't let them down!

Rushing out the door, I hear the wind chimes singing in the cool breeze. "Slow down a bit," they call after me.

Finding a shortcut through the morning traffic, I drive through a quiet neighborhood on my way to the next thing. I spot an older couple trimming and caring for their flowers with such an air of contentment about them. As I pass by, they smile and raise their hands in a friendly wave. They don't want anything from me. I'm startled by how wonderful it feels to be acknowledged just for being alive. That thought pierces my heart as tears prick my eyes. Weary, empty. I'm so tired.

As the busy morning winds down, my drive home takes me past my favorite park. Do I take a quick break and try to breathe? Pulling into a shaded spot, I step out and make my way to the bench under the tall pine trees. Quiet. Peace.

Sitting under the trees, I feel nature's healing work begin to break through and soothe the frantic, exhausted, frustrated edges of my mind, soul, and body. Your presence is here with me. I sense You in the cool air under the trees that puffs and fluffs my hair, stirring the pine branches. Whispers…

I'm allowed to just be with You here under the trees. No expectations. Your voice in the peaceful sounds of the park eases and gentles the ever-nagging feeling of heaviness from the expectations and demands on my time and energy. It pulls, strains, and tears; one can't function from an empty cup.

As I sit with You and close my tired eyes, I envision You constructing a boundary around me. It is strong, tightly woven, and beautiful. It is iridescent white. Pure. Safe. It carefully encloses me. Inside are peaceful places of rest. All the things You have created me to be and crave are here—Nature, peace, my calling. You are here. I'm protected. My energy, joy, peace, and value are guarded against those things that threaten and thrash against the boundary. I get to choose who and what enters my space. Wisdom and Discernment are faithful gatekeepers.

I watch as You repel those things not meant for me to carry and manage for others; lessons not meant for me. You shield me from the disappointment and frustration of these unmet demands, sending them out and away, no longer mine. Actually, they never were. You heal me. You restore me. You strengthen my voice.

Feeling refreshed and lighter, I head home. My time with You was kind, safe, and precious. You gave me permission to soak in Your peace and rest my weary self. Not all battles are mine to fight. Boundaries are beautiful things.

FATHER,

I pray for the one who needs Your help. The one who feels overwhelmed right now by all that life is spewing at them. It is relentless with no end in sight. They are so tired. Your child is hanging on by a thread, trying so hard to shield those that they love from the chaos and turmoil churning around them. It hurts their heart, Father, and they need relief.

Hear their prayers as they take the ounce of energy they have left and turn toward You, seeking Your face. You are the Prince of Peace. You are the ever-present lover of our souls. Thank you for responding to that small, but fiery bit of faith they lift up to you with tired arms; arms that have been working so hard to stave off the storms and protect those they hold dear. You have all authority and power.

By Your voice, Your glance, and Your will, the stormy waves still, and the chaos ceases to smother and overwhelm. At Your command, peace descends and covers the one who desperately needs to feel the heaviness lift and hear You speak to their heart and spirit that they can let go. They can release the ones they love into Your hands of protection and mercy.

Thank you that even now, the weight of all they have been carrying is lifting. Your presence covers them, healing and bringing

Your beautiful peace right into the midst of it all. Thank you for hearing our prayers and for loving us so well and so perfectly.

In the name of Jesus, our peace,
Amen

Isaiah 26:3 NIV "You will keep in perfect peace those whose minds are steadfast, because they trust in you."

I Saw You

IN THE BLUSTERY WIND, tossing treetops, and swirling flower petals in the park.

As ducks and geese glide through the choppy water, rooting and searching out tidbits and seeds in the tall reeds at the edge of the pond.

As my hair fluffed and danced at Your touch, while Nature healed and refreshed.

I saw You.

In the women walking side by side in the neighborhood, laughing and smiling together.

When the older woman working in her flower bed waved a friendly greeting.

As the little boy, walking with his grandpa, stopped to show off his fancy cowboy boots with a proud smile.

I saw You.

When the text message from a friend pops up to say, "Hi! I'm thinking of you!"

When the birds in the garden sing happy songs that lift my heart.

As the man with the Army Veteran hat picks up his coffee order and a kind person tells him that his service is appreciated, thanking him for the sacrifices he's made.

I saw You.

When a child and her mom pass by the homeless man sitting on a bench and offer him a bag with a scone from the bakery and a cup of coffee, all with a smile.

As the older gentleman walks his dog around the park, he encounters a young man who stops to chat with him and admires his dog. The loneliness that hurts his heart was kept at bay for just a little while.

When the frazzled and weary server finds the generous tip and encouraging note from a kind patron.

I saw You.

You are in all of these simple acts of kindness. In the way others help a lonely person feel seen, provide for the needs of someone who's struggling, and take a moment to brighten the day of the one who feels lost and desperate, the one who needs to know You see them. Jesus with skin on.

You are in all these moments. It may seem trivial and fleeting, but it means the world to the one You deeply love; the one who cries out to You and You answer with other people who have a heart like Yours.

I saw You today as I watched humanity respond to Your call to simple acts of kindness and compassion. For God so loved the world... *Divine Presence*. It filled my heart with hope. It blessed me.

Thaw

It starts as a tiny drip, a barely perceptible warming.

Frozen trees with branches always pointing up, up, up. Sun seekers.

Mini rivulets of icy water course down the deeply furrowed bark of the Giant Sequoias. Ancient growth and weather-worn zig zags lead downward. Life-giving water, living water.

Quiet, quiet. You might hear it softly pattering on the water-gorged forest floor.

Changing seasons and time marching on. Constant. Purpose. The circle of life presses on regardless of human chaos. Divine design—His fingerprints everywhere.

Warm, heavenly breath thaws the human heart as it emerges from a season of frozen dreams and elusive peace. The gentle warming goes unnoticed at first.

The heart seeks warmth and solace, a thaw from seasons of pain. Not unlike the towering trees, humanity is drawn to look up, seeking clarity, seeking hope. Son seekers.

Softly, the warm breath of Life hovers and embraces the frozen one. Whispers of love and safety. Gentle drops of water—life-giving, healing, hopeful—slowly flow over, through, and down the deep furrows, cracks, and hollows that left grooves and scars along the skin of the soul. Living water trickles down to the thirsty heart. New beginnings. Hope.

Tender new growth will begin its journey up, up as it seeks the Son, like nature as it thaws and raises fragile shoots and buds up to life-giving Light. Divine fingerprints everywhere.

Little Slice of Nature

THE TIPS of the fairy wings glow in the early morning sunlight. The garden statues are coated with a sheen of ice. The winter nights have been so cold, but dawn always comes.

As the sun breaks over the horizon, I see the plump outline of the small birds that sit each morning in the bare branches of the apple tree. They seem to be traveling companions; always together—watching and waiting for me to emerge with seeds and peanuts.

Next come the squirrels. I hear them rustle through the neighbor's tree as they make their way along the fence. Several sets of watchful black eyes follow me through the garden as I scatter peanuts for them and the trio of crows that spy from the phone wires a few streets over.

The hot Chai tea in my Army Mom mug steams in the early light, keeping my chilly hands warm as they peek out through the long sleeves of my thick hoodie.

I sit for a bit on my patio this morning and soak up the comfort of my garden. Peace. Contentment. Rest. It is home. The birds, squirrels, and neighborhood cats that come to visit every day are like my little wild family. My little slice of nature. Their songs, chatter, and even the scolding of the scrub jays are pleasant.

Life outside the garden gets overwhelming and exhausting. I am thankful for this bit of respite just outside my patio door. I can hear the Creator's voice, calming and soothing as I listen to the beautiful sounds of nature and drink in all the colors of His creation. Brushstrokes of love and peace scattered yet perfectly placed, bringing rest to a weary soul and abundant life to a simple suburban garden.

Slow Down

THAT FIRST PEACEFUL SLICE of a new day has a sweet and cozy feel to it. You come up out of that dreamy place of slumber, and for a few moments, all is well. You feel comfy, warm, and tucked in—calm mind and heart. But Worry and Busyness wake up too, poking and prodding at your thoughts.

"Remember to make that appointment and check your email. You still need to make that uncomfortable call. What did they mean when they said_____ and did they have a weird tone in their voice? Get to the gym!"

In the blink of your still sleepy eye, the peaceful start to your day is slowly unraveling.

Making your morning coffee, you notice the songbirds waking up with happy greetings, cheerful and unrushed. The routine of their daily search for nourishment is calming.

Sitting at the patio table with your steamy mug of French Roast, you hear nature, and its soothing rhythms call out to your soul...

Slow down a bit! Bask in the wintry sun. Warm your bones and heart. Breathe.

Slow down a bit! Soak in the joy of the wind chimes dancing in the light breeze. Let go!

Slow down a bit! Let your mind rest just a little longer. Relax.

Slow down a bit! Feel the chill of cool air on your exposed skin. Invigorating!

Slow down a bit! Breathe in the scents of the winter garden... rosemary, dry leaves, cold earth. Soothing.

It is okay to slow down. Those tasks, worries, and to-do lists will still be there, but you can face them with a calm and steady mindset infused with His peace and discernment. He goes before you, clearing the way, walks beside you helping you over the rough spots, and follows behind as your rear guard. Listen for His gentle whisper and give yourself permission to just slow down.

Jars of Clay

THE POTTER is at His wheel. All around His workroom, heavenly beings wait in expectation of the Masterpiece. Some sing in Holy languages that interweave with His words of prophesy, purpose, and love. Their songs infuse the clay with unique gifts, peace, and immense value. An impartation of Himself. Holy. Supernatural. Mystery.

His workroom is sacred. Nothing enters without His permission. Each lump of clay is precious. The Potter knows the exact purpose, place, and circumstance for each vessel He creates, and not a thing is left out, forgotten, or rushed. The Triune Potter is intentional, specific, and perfect. Every jar created reflects the time, attention, and deep love He holds for it. His vision for each jar comes to life under His masterful hands, as the scars He knew He would bear for His creation brush up against me and you.

The roughness of His scars creates slight imperfections in the clay, which are intentional and beautiful to the Potter. He permits cracks and crevices, nooks and crannies that to human eyes are faults and defects. Not to Him. These cracks and broken spots allow others to get a glimpse of Him through us. We are permeated with Him; His breath, His love, and His peace; all the unique gifts that He placed in us. Through our chips and oddities, others who are searching for Him, who may have lost their way, or are traveling in the dark, will see His Light seeping out through our chinks and nooks as a beacon of hope and rest. Opportunities to allow Him to speak through us and offer compassion, acceptance, and peace to a weary fellow traveler. May others do this for us when we find ourselves lost and in need of Light and Hope. The beauty of a broken vessel.

Corinthians 4:7 NLT "We now have this light shining in our hearts, but we ourselves are like fragile clay jars containing this great treasure. This makes it clear that our great power is from God, not from ourselves."

Listen

THERE'S A GENTLENESS to the air this morning like the wings of heaven's breath unfolding and beckoning me to come and see. It feels welcoming and kind.

The sleepy sun washes the sky with a sweet, muted palette as it peeks up over the hills. The higher it climbs, the stronger the sunbeams become, infusing the cool spring air with a tinge of warmth. It feels like comfort.

Birds show up in the garden and on tree branches. Some are solo, and others arrive in lively little flocks singing their morning salutation. Their songs and fluttering are cheerful and purposeful as they find the seeds and little bugs that make up their daily breakfast. It feels like provision.

Next come the squirrels. These garden residents are full of energy! Watching the young ones tease and chase each other as they cavort up and over the branches and along the fence is playful and freeing. It feels joyful.

As the spring sun rides higher in the pale blue sky, the yellow and black bumblebees buzz around the purple catmint and blue morning glory. Their easy drift from flower to flower is calming. It feels restful.

Wind chimes begin their melody as a little breeze picks up. It fluffs the wavy white tendrils of the gaura plant. The little white flowers look like dancing butterflies as the breeze tosses them this way and that. A fat bee lands on a flower and is swayed along with the breeze. It feels peaceful.

The way the sunlight filters through the apple tree branches casts shadows along the redwood fence. In between the shadowy outlines are soft beams of light that dapple the wood and give off a mysterious vibe; supernatural, perhaps. Tucked in and sheltered. It feels safe.

Growing along the fence line, the white jasmine perfumes the air with a calming, nostalgic scent that transports me back to younger days and lazy childhood summers. There is something so familiar and good, yet it flits and darts, not fully landing in your memory. It feels like home.

All these feelings and sensations flow from You. As You hovered over the vast darkness and spoke all that exists into life, You poured Yourself into each bit. Your love, peace, comfort, joy, and kindness. Your gentleness and warrior heart. All that You are is in every single thing. It's mysterious, perfect, fierce, and supernatural. It is all at Your command and does exactly what You call it to do.

Healing, joy, and safety come from Your whispers of love. It is threaded in and around Your creation as You speak in whispers, bird song, laughing breezes, and the healing silence of the forest.

Listen for the Whispers. Listen. There is deep healing to be found. Peace that passes human understanding. Can you hear Him calling you to Himself? He is safe. He is pure love. He is home. Just listen.

Love Gifts

As THE MOON FADES and the sun begins its ascent, the little breeze hovers over the Earth, waiting for her assignment. Every day is an exciting surprise! The Creator could send her anywhere. Some days she blows with full force! Other days, she gently flits through treetops, stirs the hair, and whispers His songs along the skin of those that He adores.

The Creator is a mysterious one. She sees His hand in all things. She watches as He leads, protects, and redirects humanity; all falling into the perfect design only He fully understands. The words and songs He speaks and sings over Creation are kind, untamed, and full of love. Sovereignty. He is absolute power, yet so gentle, merciful, and relentless toward those He pursues. She is honored to carry these precious gifts to the ones He directs her to visit. It is a joy seeking out His beloved, waiting until the exact moment to cool them with a soft puff of heaven-scented air.

Along forested paths, she carries the sounds and scents of nature to those seeking solace and refreshment for their world-weary hearts. She speaks to the trees and forest animals as she dips through branches and over nests, carrying their chirps, rustles, and chatter to ears that need sounds of peace. Oh, how well He knows their hearts.

Stiff and crisp, she sails over the ocean, creating deep swells that crest and crash along rocky shores or slow, gentle waves that shush and calm along sandy beaches. This assignment is sacred and holy, as those searching for answers and release look for hope, look for Him, in the rhythmic sound of the waves. Not only does she bring the power, fierce passion, and restful susurration of the waves, but she is entrusted with the cries, tears, and rage shouted into her gusts and eddies. Those are precious gems to the Creator. They must be handled with deep compassion and tender care. Merciful. What an honor to be entrusted with those spirit-deep fears, desires, and hope, so much hope.

Delightful are the days when she can freely dash, swirl, and ruffle through humanity, teasing, playing, and whiffling through parks, paths, and backyard patios. Carrying His gifts of healing, hope, peace, and mercy, the little breeze spreads the scent of Jasmine and apple blossoms over the one daydreaming on her patio. She needs a bit of peace. The scent is soothing and kind, allowing her mind to wander and rest.

In the city park, the little breeze sends tumbling showers of graceful, finished leaves along the twisty path. The man and his dog delight in the russets, browns, and reds of the crunchy, crackly leaves dotting the grass and pathway. It feels like hope, a time to slow down and heal for a bit.

The cool, deep air of the Redwoods, with the ancient-Earth scent of forest life, feeds the soul of the woman hiking alone. The heaviness of life weighs large and looming on her tender frame. The deep peace she feels among these Giants and the forest chatter gently lifts the weight she was never meant to carry. The little breeze caresses her face and dries the tears on her cheeks, speaking compassion, mercy, and peace carried straight from His Throne room.

Assignments complete, the little breeze floats and swirls among the clouds. Looking down over the landscape of humanity, she sees the generous love gifts she has scattered along the carefully designed tapestry of human life. His breath and presence floating and surrounding His beloved. Planned with perfect love and deep kindness. His mercy is new every morning. The little breeze gentles and rests, wondering where He will send her next.

Father,

I lift up the one who has doubts. They feel disoriented and are filled with so many questions that seem to have no answers. The discouragement feels heavy, and they fear they have lost their faith or never had it at all. Fear and panic creep in, whispering lies and half-truths.

I pray You will remind your much-loved child of all the ways You have loved, healed, and delighted them in the past. Call to mind the tender times that You enfolded them in Your wings and sheltered them from the enemy's arrows and lies. Silence the anxious panic that threatens to overwhelm them. They are safe. They are loved. How blessed they are that You understand the human heart! You are not worried or angry with their doubts and uncertainty. You welcome their questions and can handle their disappointment. It draws them toward You, even when they feel adrift. This world is harsh and exhausting, with many voices clamoring for their loyalty and attention. You lived among us. You know it is hard to be us.

I pray You will gently speak Your words of peace and deliverance over them. May they encounter You in small, sweet ways that fan the flame of faith in their soul that never truly went out, but was covered in the detritus of disappointment, frustration, and fear. You are the Healer, Redeemer, and Lover. I pray You cover this precious soul with Yourself. You are enough. You will never leave them.

In the powerful name of Jesus Christ,
Amen

Psalm 23:6 NIV "Surely your goodness and love will follow me all the days of my life, and I will dwell in the house of the Lord forever."

The Night Watchman

THE SLEEPY WORLD is winding down for the day. The ever-bright sun makes its way around the sphere of Earth as it has always done, is doing, and will continue to do until He who called it into being says, "Enough."

Heavenly bodies breathed into existence, rise and set, move and shift according to His desire. The perfect design set into motion as the Triune Creator hovered over the Earth, breathing all things into motion. Sovereign, eternal, good.

The sun's last gasp of fire and beauty fizzles and glows as the moon and stars ready themselves for their time to shine. Their light is different than that of the sun. Mysterious, deep, supernatural.

They shine and shimmer like clockwork in the night. God ordained guides. For untold centuries, travelers have relied on their precision in the sky to lead, guide, and attempt to explain the mysteries of Earth and the shadows of the unknown.

With eyes that see all and wisdom beyond understanding, the Night Watchman observes all that happens to His beloved on the spinning Earth He created. As we slip into sleep, He is aware as breathing slows and deepens, as muscles relax and eyelids flutter. He hears the sigh of our spirit and sees the restless fears that wait in the wings, hoping to bring thoughts of worry, panic, and frantic overthinking. His glance banishes them. Such joy it brings to Him when His worried one speaks His name in the still of night, asking Him to silence the voices and flood them with His peace, safety, and love.

Some of the deepest and most profound healing comes to us in the dark still of the night. When all is quiet and the mystery of Him abounds, the Night Watchman covers us with wings of healing and rest. Divine exchanges and supernatural encounters flow and swirl as Divine whispers speak and prophesy over us.

Never sleeping, ever vigilant, His staff leads, guides, and makes a way while we slumber. We can let go, relax our clenched hands, and invite thoughts of Him into our world-weary minds and bodies. Battles over us are won in heavenly places as we rest in His care and protection. All is well. The Night Watchman is near.

Psalm 4:8 NLT "In peace I will lie down and sleep, for you alone, O Lord, will keep me safe."

FATHER,

I pray for the one with unanswered prayers. They have committed to faithfully lift up the loved one, circumstance, wound, or health issue. They have been praying for a long time. Discouragement and hopelessness are scratching at the door of their heart. Disillusionment and suspicion are seeking a way into their weary spirit. They still believe, but...

It is hard to understand Your ways and will. They pray for good things and positive outcomes. However, this burden is so heavy, and they can't hear Your voice. Soul-deep exhaustion is hovering. They need a breakthrough. They want to give themselves permission to place the need into Your strong and powerful hands, but they are afraid to let go.

Will You give them a glimpse of what You are orchestrating behind the scenes? You do not rest or grow weary. Your loving eyes are on them constantly. They are never out of Your grasp. I pray for an answer, a way forward, and a resolution. I ask for healing, reconciliation, and protection. Fill this precious soul with such peace that they know they have encountered the Living God who comforts, listens, heals, and protects. Fill them with hope.

When Your answer is no or not now, it is difficult to grasp with the human mind. Please minister to them when Your answers don't match what they have prayed for. Blanket them with comfort and sing over them as You hold them tenderly. I pray that deep ministers to deep, and your weary child will let themselves rest in the sanctuary of Your presence as You work out all things for their good. You are good, kind, and compassionate. Remind them that faith the size of a mustard seed can move mountains. Strengthen them as they wait and trust in You for whatever answer You give them.

In the powerful and compassionate name of Jesus Christ,
Amen

Psalm 91:15-16 NLT "The Lord says, 'I will rescue those who love me. I will protect those who trust in my name. When they call on me, I will answer; I will be with them in trouble. I will rescue and honor them.'"

Summer

Cool mornings with coffee on the patio, I wake up with nature. Walking barefoot through the dewy grass with the warming sun on my shoulders as the first rays filter through branches. The chill on my skin is startling and refreshing! A friendly greeting to the busy bees while I fuss in the garden. Morning gives way to the afternoon heat and slowing rhythm. Creatures rest and watch from shadowy places as a slow, lazy breeze ruffles feathers, fur, and flower-heavy branches.

The day winds down as the heat of the afternoon gentles and recedes. It's the golden hour where the light lingers just a bit longer before dusk falls. Face upturned, I watch the carpet of stars appear along with the sailing moon. The moon glow casts shadows along the edges of the yard as a faint warmth radiates gently up from the sunbaked patio stones.

The backyard night visitors begin their hunting routine to the music of the cricket and tree frog symphony in the far reaches of the garden and the nearby marshy area. Sleepy, lowing drifts on the air from the cows settling down in the nearby open space. Noises of deep night flit and filter in and out of my dreams as cool breezes pour through open windows.

As summer returns with another spin of the Earth, nostalgia comes along for the ride. The familiar scent of pine trees, a whiff of lake water, and the hot earth smell reserved for summer are reminders of family picnics on the screened-in porch at my Grandparents' house. Three-bean salad, rich eggy potato salad, and fresh green beans, along with the catch from our morning fishing trip. It feels like belonging, it feels like home.

The smoky smell of neighborhood BBQs, laughter, and fire pits brings up memories of camping, beach days, and hikes in the Redwoods, where the heat of the day is kept at bay under the full canopy of branches. A gentle and serene silence as the afternoon wind sighs and whispers through the branches.

Welcoming these nostalgic feelings and sensations, I let them wash over me. You speak through creation the things You have planned for me, tinged with sweet reminders of happy times and places. All of these scents and sounds become words that You speak to me—reminders of what was, what is, and what is coming. The anticipation of a rich and lovely treasure hunt filled with Your presence and sweet surprises dances along my shoulders and teases in my hair. The wind of Your spirit brushes against my heart and tugs at my feet as You lead me through this season of brighter, longer light, blue sky, and the peace of a summer night spent with the glow of the moon and stars as my companions. And You, always and forever with me.

Can You Hear Him?

O<small>N A SUMMER NIGHT</small> when cricket symphonies lull and soothe as the moon sails high and pinprick stars wink…He whispers in dark, nocturnal rustlings with deep, supernatural words of mystery.

When the wind shushes and sighs through the Redwood canopy as you hike and soak in the forest…He whispers timeless songs of creation.

Opening your eyes as a new day starts, before the mad rush of living takes over and you savor your morning coffee…He whispers an invitation, "Come and talk with me."

As you putter in the garden, trimming and admiring the flowers…He whispers promises of new life and a season of rebirth in the rich scent of turned earth.

When the day is done and your tired body falls into those in-between moments before you drift off to sleep…He whispers words of rest and speaks to you in your dreams.

Can you hear Him?

When your heart feels heavy, you retreat to the hidden bench under the willow branches that skim over the pond… His whispers of healing and hope perfume the air around you.

When the cruel, hurtful words sting your heart, and tears spill over and down your cheeks…He whispers songs of love and belonging. He captures each tear. You are His.

As waves crash along the lonely beach and you fling your deepest needs and fears to the relentless tides…His whispers become a divine exchange, taking your hurt and giving you Himself. He is enough.

Taking that first frightening, tentative step of faith into something new and unknown…He whispers courage and strength into your mind, spirit, and body. He is with you. Worry must flee.

With pain so deep and raw that you have no words or tears left…His whispers become intercession in heavenly languages, traveling straight to the Holy of Holies.

Can you hear Him?

When loved ones are far away and your mind is full of frightening thoughts and the chaos of the unknown…He whispers safety and protection. Their names are written on the palm of His hands. He speaks peace, and fear bows.

When the world is filled with injustice, cruelty, and division… He whispers compassion and authority—He is King. There are none before Him. Alpha and Omega.

When self-reliance has taken its toll and you finally unclench your fists and cry to Him in exhaustion…He whispers gentle songs of rest and comfort. All is well, He's got this.

And...

On the lighter days, when the hurry is hushed and you sit under the apple tree, talking to Him, thanking Him, and whispering that you love Him, an incense of thankfulness, praise, and love rises and dances its way to His throne. As the sacred aroma swirls and fans around Him, He sings, shouts, and prophesies over you with blessings, peace, and joy. Can you hear Him?

FATHER,

I pray for the one who is seeking You—searching for Your guidance and compassion. Be with them as they seek and find the treasures You have hidden for them to discover throughout their day. May discernment and wisdom help them navigate what lies ahead.

I pray they will be aware of Your presence as You walk with them, hemming them in behind and before. Prepare them for all they will encounter today as they seek you with their whole heart. Give them strength and protection as they follow You, Your staff clearing the way of obstacles and things wishing to entangle and ensnare them. The day can take a drastic turn when fear engulfs and invades their heart and soul, causing their mind to spin. Please hide and shelter them with Your wings. Banish fearful thoughts the enemy pokes and prods them with, and fill them with Your peace.

Father, remind Your child that just the whisper of Your name causes a shift in the heavenlies beyond anything they can imagine. You never leave them; You never forsake them. Your promises are sure and solid.

Thank you for being all-powerful, yet full of compassion. Give them patience and a holy determination as they seek Your face and navigate this day. May they lean on You and bask in the songs of love You sing over them. Those who seek You will find You.

In the name of Jesus Christ our Shepherd,
Amen

Jeremiah 29:13 NLT "If you look for me wholeheartedly, you will find me."

Acknowledgements

DIVINE PRESENCE... took shape as God spoke the words from His heart to my pen...

Thank you to:

My family (Paul, Emma, Josh, Mom, Dad, and Nicole) for the feedback, encouragement, and prayers.

Wendy Moon, Tina Harrell, Jainell Gaitan, Heather Greaves, Archna Haylock, Kathryn Dunn, April White, and Kellie Johnson, for your friendship, prayers, encouragement, and feedback as *Divine Presence...* took shape.

My military mamas! Ana, Andrea, Ann, April, Archna, Jaime, Julie, Kandi, Karen, Kellie, Leyda, Maria, Megan, Peri, Sherri, Stephanie, Tina, and Tracy. Each of you are a blessing to me with your encouragement, shared tears, and humor in this crazy season of life. You are brave and courageous women whom I'm honored to call friends.

The talented women who transform my musings into books I am proud to send into the world. Pia Edberg for editing and sharpening up my words and thoughts so the voice of my book is heard, Jessie Cunniffe for bringing those words together into a beautiful blurb that draws you in, and Karolina Wudniak for creating illustrations and cover designs that perfectly capture the soul and essence of my books.

You are all appreciated!

Author Bio

MELISSA GIOMI, author of *Divine Encounters...*, *Divine Appointments...*, *Divine Whispers...*, and *Divine Presence...* is a Northern California native, born in Redding. She lives near San Francisco with her husband and their pets. They have two adult children.

Melissa is passionate about Jesus, nature, writing, and gardening. She enjoys good coffee, mornings spent on the patio, meaningful conversations, and volunteering with a local food distribution non-profit. Melissa and her husband enjoy trying new restaurants, relaxing by the ocean, hiking, and camping in the Redwoods.

Walking with God through life's seasons, Melissa believes wholeheartedly that His presence is everywhere. He is always speaking to us, delighting us, and healing us through nature, other people, and His whispers in the wind.